MYSELF TODAY

By Karen Giesbrecht

Illustrated By Jenny Nazarova

Copyright © 2018 by Karen Giesbrecht

No part of this book may be reproduced in any form without written permission, except for brief quotations in critical reviews.

Published by:

Mill Lake Books
Abbotsford, BC Canada

www.coggins.ca

Printed by Lightning Source/IngramSpark, distributed by Ingram
ISBN 978-0-9951983-5-7

For one of the most imaginative
Little Ones I know, and for all who are
teaching me about resilience.

This is Belle.

Belle loves to be hugged
and tickled.

Belle loves to play hide-and-seek with her daddy's keys.

Belle loves to wash dishes.

Belle loves cucumbers, hummus,
and quesadillas with cheese.

But some days Belle is just not herself.

Some days she is a superhero who rescues lost kittens.

Some days she is an engineer who builds train tracks as big as a coffee table.

Some days she is an explorer who can climb to the top of her daddy's shoulders.

Most of the time Belle is joyful and playful and makes everyone around her smile.

But some of the time Belle is a Harumph.

Sometimes she cries and stomps her feet and says, "No! No! No! No!"

Sometimes Belle's daddy does not know why she is a Harumph.

Maybe it is because she is hungry.

Maybe it is because she feels upset.

Maybe Belle is simply tired.

Everyone can be a Harumph when they are hungry, upset, lonely, or tired.

Sometimes, we do not realize
we are feeling these ways.

So when we do, we may need a snack.
And to talk to someone about how we feel.
Then a hug. And some quiet time.

And then we become ourselves again.
Or we can be anything
our imagination lets us be.

HUMMUS OR BEAN DIP

Blend 2 cups of cooked (or canned) chickpeas, or other legume such as edamame, lentils, white, navy, black, or kidney beans with about 1/4 cup liquid. Use a combination of olive oil, lemon juice, lime juice, water and/or soya sauce to make your dip the desired consistency. Season with salt and pepper, plus other ingredients for flavour. Traditional hummus has garlic and tahini. Also try adding roasted bell peppers or carrots, grilled onions, olives, sun dried tomatoes, avocado, feta cheese, pesto, spinach, cumin, pine nuts, cilantro, basil, and/or other herbs and spices.

USE THESE SNACKS FOR DIPPING:

- Apple Wedges
- Bell Pepper Strips
- Carrot Sticks
- Crackers
- Cucumber Coins
- Pretzels
- Toasted Pita Bread
- Tortilla Chips

Author's Bio

Karen Giesbrecht went to school to learn about good food, and now spends her time ensuring that the people she meets eat well and can continue to be creative and imaginative. At home in Vancouver, Canada, Karen is a registered dietitian who takes great delight in sharing good meals with family, friends, and those in her community who are hungry.

Illustrator's Bio

Jenny Nazarova went to school to learn to be an architect, and also uses her creativity for illustrations and other design projects. She finds that looking at the world through the eyes of a child helps her continue to see the fairy tales all around us. At home in England, Jenny takes great delight in the miracles she can design with her hands.

www.ingramcontent.com/pod-product-compliance
Lightning Source LLC
Chambersburg PA
CBHW061155010526
44118CB00027B/2982